ACHIEVING YOUR DREAMS WITH RESILIENCE

SECRET STRATEGIES FOR OVERCOMING OBSTACLES

DR. JAGADEESH PILLAI

Made with ♥ on the Notion Press Platform
www.notionpress.com

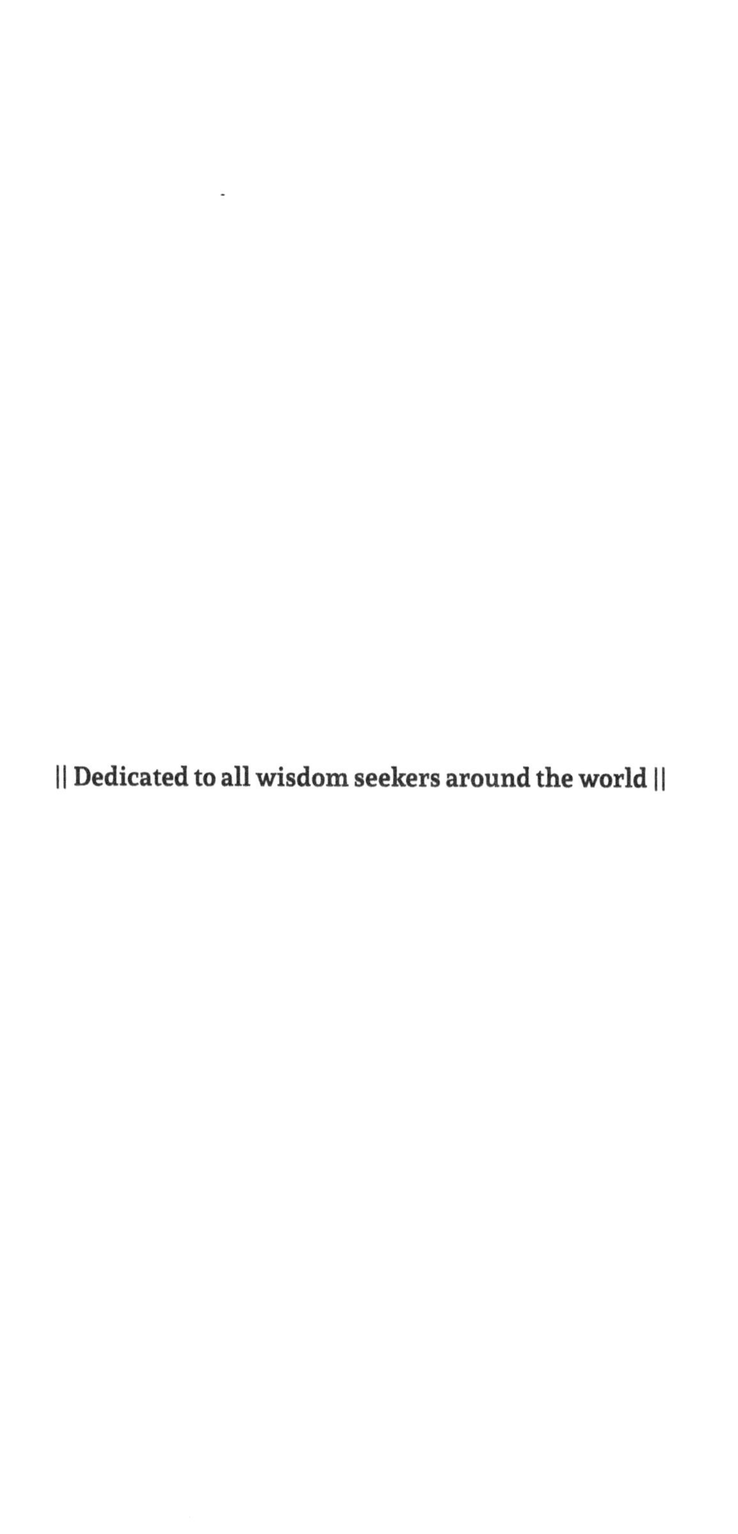

|| Dedicated to all wisdom seekers around the world ||

Contents

Contents

PRAYER

**"Om Bhadram Karnebhih Shrunuyaama
DevaahBhadram Pashyemaakshabhiryajatraah
SthirairangaistushtuvaamsastanoobhihVyashema
Devahitam YadaayuhSwasti Na Indro
VridhashravaahSwasti Nah Pooshaa
VishwavedaahSwasti Nastaarkshyo ArishtanemihSwasti
No Brihaspatir DadhaatuOm Shantih, Shantih, Shantih"**

The literal meaning of this mantra is: OM. O Gods! Let us
hear auspicious words from our ears. O reverent Gods! Let
us behold propitious visions from our eyes, let our organs
and body be stable, healthy, and strong. Let us do that
which is pleasing to the gods in the life span allotted to us.
May Indra, inscribed in the scriptures, bring us fortune!
May Pushan, the knower of the world, grant us prosperity!
May Trakshya, who vanquishes enemies, bestow us with
blessings! May Brihaspati bring us success!
OM Peace, Peace, Peace.

About the Author

Dr. Jagadeesh Pillai is a renowned Guinness World Record holder, writer, and researcher hailing from Varanasi, also known as the abode of Lord Shiva. With a Ph.D. in Vedic Science and a range of creative ideas and achievements, he is a true polymath. He is the author of more than 100 books including Research Publications. Although his roots can be traced back to Kerala, the people of Varanasi hold him in high regard and affectionately consider him one of their own.

Dr. Pillai has achieved four Guinness World Records in the following subjects:

"Script to Screen" - In this record, Dr. Pillai produced and directed an animation film within the shortest time possible, breaking the previous record set by Canadians. He has also received numerous national and international awards and recognitions for this achievement.

Longest Line of Postcards - For this record, Dr. Pillai created a line of 16,300 postcards on the occasion of the 163rd anniversary of Indian Postal Day. The event also included a questionnaire about the Indian flag.

Largest Poster Awareness Campaign - Dr. Pillai designed an awareness campaign on the subject of "Beti Bachao - Beti Padhao" (Save the Girl Child - Educate the Girl Child) to achieve this record.

Largest Envelope - In tribute to the Indian Prime Minister's

"Make in India" initiative, Dr. Pillai created a 4000 square meter envelope using waste paper to achieve this record.

Attempted - **70000 Candles on a 210 kg Cake** - To celebrate the 70th Indian Independence Day, Dr. Pillai attempted to light 70,000 candles on a 210 kg cake, which was recorded in World Records India.

Attempted - **Documentary on Dhamek Stupa of Sarnath in 17 Languages** - Dr. Pillai attempted to create a documentary on the Dhamek Stupa of Sarnath, dubbing it in 17 different languages. The result of this attempt is currently awaiting confirmation from the Guinness World Records.

Dr. Pillai is skilled in teaching the Bhagavad Gita, a Hindu scripture, and is popular among young people. He has helped many young people improve their lives through his motivational teachings.

In addition to teaching, he has composed and sung numerous Sanskrit Bhajans and patriotic songs.

He has also written and directed several short films and documentaries for awareness campaigns, and has volunteered with the police in both UP and Kerala to spread awareness about various issues through videos and photography.

Incredibly, he has produced and directed over 100 documentaries about the city of Varanasi, all on his own.

He has also helped and guided more than 25 boys and girls to achieve world records through creative and innovative methods. He is a multifaceted person who uses his intellect and the blessings given to him by God to excel in various areas. He is both a teacher and a student, always learning and teaching, and is able to master any subject he comes across.

He is a selfless social activist and motivational speaker who has overcome struggles and failures to become a successful and enthusiastic individual with a rich life experience.

In addition to his work with the Bhagavad Gita, he is also an efficient Tarot card reader, Astro-Vastu consultant, and a talented singer and composer. He has sung the entire Ram Charita Manas and Bhagavad Gita in his own compositions, and has sung the phrase "Lokah Samastha Sukhino Bhavantu" in 50 different languages. He is currently working on a detailed and scientific study of Vedas, Upanishads, Puranas, and the Bhagavad Gita. He has also composed and sung the Hanuman Chalisa and Gayatri Mantra in 108 and 1008 different compositions, respectively.

Awards - Four Times Guinness World Records, Winner of Mahatma Gandhi Vishwa Shanti Puraskar, Mahatma Gandhi Global Peace Ambassador, Kashi Ratna Award, Dr. APJ Abdul Kalam Motivational Person of the Year 2017, Mother Teresa Award, Indira Gandhi Priyadarshini Award, Bharat Vikas Ratna Award, Udyog Ratna Award, Vigyan Prasar Award, Poorvanchal Ratn Samman.

PREFACE

In this book, "Achieving Your Dreams with Resilience: Secret Strategies for Overcoming Obstacles," we will explore the power of resilience and how it can help you achieve your dreams. Resilience is the ability to bounce back from adversity, and it is a vital trait for anyone who wants to achieve their goals and live a fulfilling life.

This book is for anyone who has ever felt discouraged by obstacles and setbacks, or for those who want to build their resilience to better handle the challenges that come their way. It is for those who want to learn the secret strategies for overcoming obstacles and achieving their dreams.

We will cover a wide range of topics including identifying and overcoming self-limiting beliefs, building a support system, setting SMART goals, managing stress and emotions, learning from failure, building mental and physical strength, the power of positive thinking and gratitude, overcoming procrastination and staying motivated, building resilience in the face of adversity, the importance of self-care, learning to adapt and be flexible, the role of mindfulness, the power of persistence and determination.

This book will provide you with the tools you need to overcome obstacles, build resilience, and achieve your dreams. It is my hope that by reading this book, you will gain the confidence and motivation to take action and make your dreams a reality.

෪

I

Understanding Resilience & Its Importance for Achieving Your Dreams

Resilience is a word that is often used to describe people who have gone through hardships and yet have been able to pick themselves back up again and continue reaching for their dreams. Resilience is a type of personal strength, the ability to adapt and change while still pushing forward despite challenging circumstances. It is a critical aspect of achieving success, and it is essential to understand how resilience works and how to cultivate it in order to remain focused on achieving one's goals.

The first step in understanding resilience is to acknowledge that sometimes life will not turn out exactly as planned. In fact, it is quite common for individuals to face obstacles even when taking action towards their dreams. Taking setbacks in stride and continuing to move forward is the primary element of resilience. It is important to identify that a setback does not mean a complete failure, but rather a necessary lesson to be learned in order to move forward. As such, resilient individuals are those who are able to recognize that failure may be part of the process and who are still able to maintain motivation.

There are a few key steps that can be taken in order to cultivate resilience. Firstly, it is important to remain positive and recognize that failure and mistakes are a normal, inevitable part of achieving success. Keeping a balanced perspective can also be useful, as this helps to put life into perspective and to understand that any such setback is only temporary. Additionally, taking time to practice self-care can be incredibly beneficial in terms of keeping the stress levels manageable and maintaining resilience. Lastly, seeking out support from others can be helpful in times of need.

Having a strong sense of resilience is essential for achieving one's dreams. Resilience is crucial in terms of staying grounded and motivated despite any challenges that may arise. Understanding how to cultivate resilience and using it to one's advantage can make all the difference in achieving long-term success.

"*The future belongs to those who believe in
the beauty of their dreams.*"

- Eleanor Roosevelt

☙

II

Identifying and Overcoming Self-Limiting Beliefs

We all have beliefs that form our behavior and guide us in life, but those beliefs sometimes become limiting and can harm our progress. Self-limiting beliefs can take many forms and can hold us back in our daily lives. It is important to understand these beliefs, identify them, and find practical ways to overcome them in order to move forward and live our best lives.

First and foremost, understanding self-limiting beliefs requires that we identify them. To do this, we must pay attention to both our conscious thoughts and our unconscious behaviors. It can be helpful to become aware of our thought patterns and the way that we talk to ourselves. Often the way that we talk to ourselves can be quite self-limiting and create anxiety and fear, preventing us from doing our best. Additionally, many of us often pay attention to our failures more than our successes. We may feel like failures when we don't measure up to expectations, or if we are unable to accomplish something. In doing so, we can start to believe that we are not capable of achieving our goals and objectives.

Once we have become aware of the self-limiting beliefs that are holding us back, we can begin to work on overcoming them. It can help to focus on the present and to accept our feelings. A key to overcoming self-limiting beliefs is to be kind to ourselves and to practice self-forgiveness. It can be helpful to challenge our own thoughts and to focus on the most positive aspects rather than the negative ones. Additionally, it can be beneficial to practice relaxation techniques, such as deep breathing, to help reduce stress and anxiety levels.

Moreover, it can be useful to create a supportive environment that encourages growth. Surrounding ourselves with positive people who are supportive of our goals and ambitions can help us to stay focused on our desired outcome. We can also create external structures that provide us with an additional sense of security and stability.

Finally, self-reflection is an important practice for understanding our thoughts and emotions and for challenging our self-limiting beliefs. We must reflect deeply on the beliefs that we hold and work to create new, healthier beliefs that will guide us in life.

In conclusion, self-limiting beliefs can sometimes hold us back in life and prevent us from achieving our goals and objectives. To overcome these beliefs, it is important to pay attention to our thoughts and behaviors, be kind to ourselves, and create a supportive environment. We must also practice self-reflection and challenge our own thoughts and beliefs in order to create new, healthier beliefs that will guide us in life.

"If you can dream it, you can do it."

- Walt Disney

&

III

Building a Support System for Resilience

Building a Support System for Resilience is an important part of achieving success in life. A resilient person is someone who is able to adapt and respond positively to challenging situations, often coming out on top. A support system is any group of people who can provide emotional, physical, or other forms of assistance to help someone achieve a specific goal. In order to build a support system that encourages resilience, it is important to identify those individuals in your life who can provide the necessary support.

Friends, family, and professionals such as counselors, pastors, or psychologists are all people who can be tapped into for support when needed. These individuals can serve as a sounding board in times of need and provide objective advice when needed. Additionally, asking one or two close friends to be part of your support system can be beneficial, as they are likely to be honest and provide objective feedback.

It is also important to create a positive mindset in order to stay resilient. Positive self-talk and affirmation of one's own strengths can help to stay resilient in challenging times. Building a foundation of self-care is also essential for staying resilient. Taking time for hobbies, physical activities, and other forms of relaxation can help to keep up energy and motivation levels.

Finally, having a plan of action in place to address problems is instrumental in staying resilient. Having a list of things to do when facing difficult situations can help to lessen stress and provide a sense of control. This can include journaling, talking through the issue with someone you trust, or making a plan for how to strategize and resolve the problem.

Overall, building a support system for resilience is key to achieving success in life. By identifying people and professionals in your life who can provide emotional and physical support, having a positive mindset, and creating a plan of action to address issues, anyone can build a support system and become more resilient.

"A dream doesn't become reality through magic; it takes sweat, determination, and hard work."

- Colin Powell

IV

Setting SMART Goals & Creating A Plan For Achieving Dreams

For individuals aspiring to achieve their dreams in life, the importance of smart goal setting and the creation of a plan to achieve those goals cannot be understated. By using the SMART framework of goal-setting, one can set a vision for their goals, create an actionable plan for achieving them, and push themselves to reach the desired outcome. The mnemonic SMART stands for Specific, Measurable, Achievable, Realistic, and Timely; and all of these elements of goal-setting should be taken into account when creating a plan to achieve one's dreams.

The process of setting SMART goals should begin by being clear and concise about the specific goal they wish to achieve. The goal should be specific and well defined, as a vague and unclear goal can lead to aimless action. For example, someone wishing to become a successful entrepreneur should address what business they will run and how they expect to make money. Clarifying specifics of the dream, such as the target markets, funding sources, products or services they will provide, etc., can be beneficial to lay the foundation of a plan to achieve the goal.

The next step in the SMART framework is to make the goals measurable; that is, one should decide in advance what measurements they will use to determine when the goal has been achieved. In the case of an entrepreneurial goal, measurable elements might include a certain number of sales, profitability, or performance benchmarks. Defining metrics to measure success empowers one to track the progress they are making toward their goals.

After establishing the specifics and measurements of a goal, aspiring achievers should then assess the goals they have set, and ensure they are achievable. This includes realistically assessing the resources that one has available, such as time, money, personnel, skills, etc., and understanding if these resources are sufficient to accomplish the desired outcome. Setting an achievable goal ensures that the action taken towards that goal is directed in the right manner, and will result in potential success.

The fourth element of SMART goals is to ensure that the goals are realistic. Unless one is an idealist, it is important to ensure that the goals one sets are practical, and can be reasonably accomplished. Dreaming big is important, but without a realistic plan for achieving those dreams, they can remain lofty aspirations.

The final element of the SMART framework is to set deadlines and milestones that are time-sensitive. Many aspirers can make the mistake of setting a goal but not giving themselves an end date or any other deadlines or milestones along the way. Certain goals that require lots of small steps to complete may benefit from breaking them down into sections and assigning deadlines or checkpoints to each one. This way, the accomplishment of the most important steps can be made sure with a sense of urgency.

Once the goal has been broken down into smaller, achievable steps, it is important to set deadlines and milestones that are time-sensitive. This will help ensure that the most important steps are completed with a sense of urgency. Additionally, setting deadlines and milestones can help to keep the goal-setter motivated and on track to achieving their goal.

"The only thing that will stop you from
fulfilling your dreams is you."

- Tom Bradley

V

Managing Stress and Emotions for Resilience

Managing stress and emotions are key elements in achieving dreams. Resilience is the ability to cope with difficult times and to recover quickly. Having strong resilience means that it is easier to stay focused and to take on and succeed at difficult tasks. Developing this resilience is essential when approaching any big dream.

First and foremost, effective stress management is essential to achieving dreams. Stress can be overwhelming, but by taking intentional steps to recognize and manage it, we can reclaim our lives from the feeling of being stuck. A great way to start is to identify triggers and possible solutions. For example, if a situation or interaction makes you feel overwhelmed, can you avoid it in the future? Can you learn to express yourself and communicate your feelings better?

Once stressors have been identified, a variety of techniques can be used to manage them. Aside from the basic needs such as diet, exercise, and sleep, relaxation techniques such as meditation, controlled breathing, journaling and progressive muscle relaxation have been shown to have positive effects on stress levels. Additionally, reaching out to a friend or therapist can provide additional coping strategies.

Another factor in achieving dreams is managing emotions. It can be tempting to wallow in negative emotions, leading to a lack of motivation and self-defeating thoughts. The first step to effectively managing emotions is to recognize and accept them. Instead of trying to push them away or suppress them, it is important to acknowledge what is happening on the inside and explore how you can work with it.

Once emotions are being handled effectively, it is easier to focus on a goal and take action. Positive affirmations, goal setting, and visualization are all effective strategies for staying on track. When difficult emotions arise, it is important to pause and reflect on what is helpful to handle the situation well.

In conclusion, stress and emotion management are important tools for resilience and achieving dreams. Being able to recognize the sources of stress and emotions and come up with strategies to manage them is essential. With practice and dedication, anyone can become more resilient and find the strength to make their dreams come true.

• 23 •

"The only way to make your dreams come true is to wake up."

- Paul Valery

VI

Learning from Failure and Moving Forward

Failure is one of the commonest and greatest of challenges that every human being on earth goes through at one point or another in their lives. We may feel disappointed and discouraged by it but in truth failure also provides us with a valuable opportunity to learn, grow and eventually reach our dreams and goals.

The journey towards achieving our dreams is often filled with many challenges, hurdles, and failures; however, it is the never give up attitude that helps us move on, continue to work hard, learn from failures and eventually succeed. When we experience failure in our lives, it tends to give us a feeling of disappointment, humiliation and discouragement. But what is important is to remember that every failure comes with valuable lessons- ones which will help us effectively tackle future challenges.

By understanding and realizing the lessons that life's experiences offer us, we can learn from our failures and view them as opportunities for personal growth and development. Every failure should be seen as a stepping stone to success, as an opportunity to learn from mistakes and do better next time. We should never allow our failures to drag us down or keep us from trying again. Failures should be seen as the way to get a clearer and better understanding of our true potential. It should also be remembered that failure should not be seen as a complete failure if one rises up and start again.

Each individual has the opportunity to create a personal plan of action to help them keep going, no matter how many times they fail. This plan can be made with the intention of identifying the causes of their failure and any areas of weakness that could be improved upon. This plan of action should include goal setting, effectively managing your schedule, and finding successful strategies to stay focused and motivated. Building up strong resilience and perseverance along with seeking the help of a supportive community will also go a long way in helping you achieve your dreams.

Overall, failure is an unavoidable part of life, learning from these experiences and using that knowledge to reach for greater heights is the key to moving forward and achieving one's dreams. Each disappointment should be seen as an opportunity to learn and develop life-long skills that will eventually build the blocks for success. Flexibility and resilience is the key to be successful in life and the realization of our dreams can help us persevere and be resilient in the face of failure.

"The only limit to our realization of tomorrow will be our doubts of today."

- Franklin D. Roosevelt

৪৩

VII

Building Mental & Physical Strength for Resilience

The capacity to stay resilient in life depends greatly on building, maintaining, and strengthening one's physical and mental health. Resilience is defined as the capacity to recover quickly from difficulties. Staying strong in the face of adversity requires both physical and psychological capabilities, and cultivating these strengths helps to create a powerful base from which to live life with contentment and joy.

Physically, resilience is developed through regular exercise. This can include any number of activities, from running to swimming to rock climbing. Regular exercise releases endorphins, which promote feelings of wellness, satisfaction and contentment. Exercise also helps to develop strength that can provide support in tougher moments and keep one centered through emotional upheaval. Additionally, regular physical activity contributes to a strong cardiovascular system, providing the energy and willpower needed to stay focused and keep going in the face of difficulty.

Mentally, resilience is developed through a combination of self-regulation and mindfulness. Self-regulation is the ability to control one's emotions in order to stay focused and productive. Ultimately, self-regulation leads to greater emotional intelligence, and can enable one to make decisions based on what is beneficial in the long term, as opposed to making decisions based on one's immediate emotional reaction. Moreover, mindfulness is the capacity to become aware of one's thoughts and feelings in the moment, without getting carried away by them or prevented from putting them into action. Mindfulness helps foster strength and a sense of inner peace and awareness, enabling one to stay calm and focused in any situation.

Furthermore, developing resilience involves expanding one's spiritual practice. This can mean anything from regular meditation to daily affirmations and mantras. Establishing a spiritual practice helps boost resilience and open one up to a higher source of strength. Spiritual practice can provide a sense of comfort and security in challenging moments and keep one mindful of what is truly important.

In conclusion, cultivating mental and physical strength are

essential components of resilience. Regular exercise, self-regulation, mindfulness and a spiritual practice are key components of developing and maintaining resilience. Ultimately, these practices lead to greater inner peace, strength, and the capacity to stay resilient no matter what life throws one's way.

*"The only thing that stands between you and
your dream is the will to try and the belief
that it is actually possible."*

- Joel Brown

VIII

The Power of Positive Thinking & Gratitude

The power of positive thinking and gratitude have been recognized for centuries as powerful tools for achieving one's dreams and desires. This philosophy holds that if you fill your life with the positive energy of good thoughts, maintain a mindset of appreciation for what life and the universe rewards us with, then we can draw the strength and confidence necessary to accomplish greatness. This concept is especially helpful when attempting to pursue our highest dreams and desires and can be applied in several different ways.

Positive thinking is not just about believing and dreaming big, but also about taking action. Having a positive attitude and mindset can lead you to tap into creative solutions that haven't been explored and inspire you to work hard. When you truly believe you can and will make your vision a reality, the possibilities are infinite, and the energy to pursue them is all around you.

Gratitude also plays a major role in this philosophy. Showing appreciation for your current circumstances in life and the small victories, no matter how insignificant, can help keep your morale higher for longer than if you only focus on the end goal. It helps propel you to stay motivated and thankful for the adventure along the way.

Last but not least, keeping this positive energy and sense of gratitude close at hand gives you the right kind of energy which you will later be able to use in support of achieving your dreams. The power of positive thinking and gratitude is a powerful tool that can help you make the vision a reality and turn dreams into realities.

When these two concepts are integrated into your daily practice, they act as a form of self-empowerment and can strengthen the relationship you have with yourself. This self-empowerment can propel you along the journey of achieving your goals and dreams, allowing you to remain positive, focused, and driven on your quest for greatness.

Overall, the power of positive thinking and gratitude is a powerful practice which, when implemented correctly and adhered to, can manifest beautiful results in your life and help you reach your goals and dreams. These two concepts are instrumental in maintaining the momentum needed to keep pushing forward until that desired end result is reached.

છ

"The only way to do great work is to love what you do."

- Steve Jobs

൹

IX

Overcoming Procrastination & Staying Motivated

Procrastination can be a dream killer. It's easy to get caught up in social media, television, and other distractions. Feeling overwhelmed is a common feeling, and it can make it easy for people to "put off" an activity for another day. It can be challenging to stay motivated enough to achieve the goals and dreams we have for ourselves.

The first step in overcoming procrastination is to clearly identify the goals and dreams that you want to accomplish. It's important to focus on things that are important to you and to make a plan for achieving those goals. Once you've identified what you want to achieve, break it down into small and measurable tasks. By breaking down your goals into smaller tasks, they will be more manageable and easier to stay motivated in their pursuit. Visualizing your goals and dreams can help with staying motivated, so make sure to include visual elements in your plan.

The next step is to create an action plan that maps out the different steps you need to take in order to reach your goal. Your action plan should include a timeline with specific goals and deadlines that you can track your progress against. This can help keep you motivated and focused on what needs to be done.

The third step is to focus on the big picture. Instead of focusing on the individual tasks that need to be done, think about the entire journey that you're about to embark on. Visualizing the end goal can be a powerful motivator, and it can give you the drive and determination to keep going.

Finally, find sources of motivation and accountability. This can be anything from positive affirmations, friends and family, or co-workers. Positive encouragers and accountability partners can help you stay inspired and driven to keep going and achieve your goals.

With the right plan of action and a strong support system, overcoming procrastination and staying motivated to win dreams is possible. By setting clear goals and mapping out a plan of action to achieve them, anyone can set themselves up for success. Establishing these systems of motivation and accountability is key to success, and they are important tools in making sure that dreams don't just stay dreams, but become reality.

❧

"*The only thing that will stop you from achieving your dreams is fear of failure.*"

- Eric Thomas

୫

X

Building Resilience in the Face of Adversity

Dealing with adversity can be difficult and overwhelming, but building resilience gives us the strength to stand up to the challenges we face and find new, creative pathways to keep pushing forward. Resilience is the ability to persist in the face of hardship, to stay committed in the face of opposition and to keep pushing towards one's goals despite facing obstacles. Resilience allows people to handle their hardships, learn from their mistakes, and navigate the ever-changing world with confidence and courage.

The path to building resilience begins by understanding our own strengths and weaknesses, recognizing and embracing our emotions, and finding ways to combat the anxiety that can come with facing difficult moments. It is essential for us to be conscious of what motivates us, and to create meaningful connections between our goals and our values. Knowing ourselves and our true interests and goals helps to give us the mental clarity and momentum to face any rivals.

The next step to developing resilience is to accept that difficulties come with life. Adversity is a part of life, and it's unavoidable. That's why it's important to learn how to work through the difficult moments and to build up the strength to keep going. Learning how to cope with difficulties comes from recognizing and accepting uncomfortable emotions, taking a step back to observe our thoughts, and understanding how to maintain a positive outlook despite difficult circumstances.

Continued practice in a lot of these areas helps to build resilience and sets us up to reach our dreams. To achieve our dreams, striving for personal growth is essential. We must seize each day, take initiative, and practice self-care. As we move forward we must cultivate resilience despite whatever obstacles arise.

Most importantly, when faced with a seemingly insurmountable challenge, one must remember to embrace the process, embrace the difficulty, embrace the opportunity to learn and develop our strengths along the way. With perseverance, hard work and a resilient attitude, any dream can be accomplished. Despite any difficulty, one must believe in themselves and keep pushing forward with the courage and strength to reach their goals.

"The only thing that will make your dreams
come true is hard work and dedication."

- Kobe Bryant

೮౩

XI

The Importance of Self-Care for Resilience

Self-care is the practice of taking an active role in protecting one's own well-being and happiness. In the hustle and bustle of modern life, it is all too easy to let the stress of daily activities overtake our lives, leaving us feeling overtaxed and off-balance. Self-care is a tool to help us maintain wellness, resilience and peace of mind. It is also an important part of realizing our dreams.

The importance of self-care for resilience is its ability to help us recover from and react to difficult situations. It ensures that we have the strength and energy to cope with the challenges we face. Realizing a dream often takes more effort and involves more failures than anticipated. The key to success is being able to persistently persist through the difficulties and setbacks. Self-care helps us remain mentally, physically and emotionally resilient, so that we can manage these challenges effectively and overcome them.

It is important to remember that self-care is much more than just eating healthy food, going for a run or taking a nap. It is building and maintaining healthy habits that support us in times of strain. This may include practicing mindfulness exercises to calm and manage stress, learning relaxation techniques such as yoga or tai chi to manage physical and mental tension and avoiding toxic relationships or activities. Regular activities such as walking or sports can increase both physical and mental well-being.

On a deeper level self-care is providing ourselves with the space to reflect and to nurture our inner self. Creating moments to relax away from our technological tools, to reflect on our goals and dreams, to cultivate our creativity and broaden our horizons are essential for growth. Furthermore it is important to take a break from time to time to check-in with ourselves and assess our progress. This helps to ensure that we stay on track and aligned with our values and our dreams.

In conclusion, self-care is essential for the development of physical and mental resilience necessary to realize our dreams. Self-care not only involves activities to fortify physical and mental well-being, but also offers a space to reflect and nurture our inner self. With self-care we can protect our well-being, build resilience and persistently persist in realizing our dreams.

∞

"The only way to achieve the impossible is to
believe it is possible."

- Charles Kingsleigh

ॐ

XII

Learning to Adapt and Be Flexible

In life, the reality is that having a dream and working hard to achieve it is a good way to find success and happiness. However, almost everything in life comes with some degree of unpredictability, and as such, it is important for us to learn to adapt and be flexible in pursuit of our dreams.

One reason why adaptability and flexibility are so important is that it can help ensure that even if the situation changes, you still don't give up on your dream. The truth is that the path to success is rarely the same for everyone, and the only way to overcome the difficulties that come our way is to remain open-minded, try to understand the challenges and make sure to come up with necessary changes. This skill of making quick and informed changes to our plans is essential for us to take the detours that life brings along our path to success.

Adaptability also gives us the courage to take risks and look at challenges as opportunities. Instead of getting frustrated and overwhelmed by the changes, we can use them to our advantage. Being flexible means learning to recognize when our old strategies aren't working and being able to assess our current situation and come up with new and more effective solutions. This doesn't necessarily mean changing our goals and plans, just adjusting to the changing times and working towards our dreams, in spite of the uncertainly.

It is also important to remember that the journey to success is ultimately a personal one and not everyone applies the same road map or takes the same approach to success. We all have our own individual skills and strengths and therefore we adapt, learn and adjust according to our specific context and needs. This also implies that giving up is not an option and that we have to have the resilience and strength to take risks and continuously experiment with different strategies.

In summary, learning to be flexible and adaptive is an essential skill to have if we are going to take the unpredictable journey to success. It gives us the courage to take risks, try new strategies, and look for the opportunities that life has to offer. As such, being able to go with the flow and pivot according to the changing times can be the difference between failure and success.

"The only way to make your dreams a reality
is to wake up and do something about it."

XIII

The Role of Mindfulness in Resilience

Mindfulness is a concept that has become increasingly popular in recent years that involves living in the present moment, rather than worrying or dwelling on the past or future too much. Although it's often associated with mental wellbeing, it can also have a huge role in allowing people to be more resilient in order to achieve their dreams.

One way mindfulness can be beneficial for those striving to achieve their dreams is through its ability to help people be more aware of their thoughts and feelings. Too often we can be stuck thinking a certain way or being bogged down by our emotions, such as stress or worry. Mindfulness allows us to take a step back and acknowledge what we're feeling as well as why, then ask ourselves how we can move forward in a positive, productive way. It also has the potential to reduce the impact of negative thoughts and can help people find a more constructive approach to their goals which can result in greater resilience.

Mindfulness also increases our ability to notice our connection to the world around us, including our environment, our relationships, and even our passions.Being aware of these relationships can bring about a stronger sense of purpose and Passion, which can help people stay motivated during difficult times and stay engaged in tasks for a longer period of time. Knowing what our goals are, and why we are striving towards them,can make it easier to stay on track, especially during times of stress or fear.

In addition, mindfulness can increase creativity, allowing us to come up with creative problem solving strategies during difficult times. Creativity is an important factor for resilience, as it can help us think outside the box and come up with solutions to boost our confidence and commitment when we have lost our way.

When working on long term goals, we can also use mindfulness to help maintain balance in every area of our life. It can give us space to focus on positive activities, especially if our goals are taking a lot of our time and energy. By giving us the opportunity to take care of our physical, emotional and mental health, we will be better equipped to build our resilience and overcome any challenges that come our way. Additionally, engaging in mindful activities can give us a break from pushing ourselves, which can be beneficial in preventing burnout and allowing us to keep pushing towards our dreams.

Overall, mindfulness is an incredibly powerful tool in improving resilience, especially for those aiming to achieve their dreams. By allowing us to become more aware of our thoughts, feelings, and connections to the world, we can use mindfulness to stay motivated and creative even during challenging times. It can also help us stay balanced and prevent us from burning out, all of which are essential for resilience and success in the long term.

"The only way to achieve greatness is to be
willing to sacrifice today for a better
tomorrow."

૪૩

XIV

The Power of Persistence & Determination

Persistence and determination are essential qualities of successful people. Without them, it is difficult to achieve any level of accomplishment. To possess these qualities requires internal strength, courage, and an unwavering commitment to your dreams.

The power of persistence and determination allows us to stay focused on a goal and to move past any obstacles that may stand in our way. It is the determination to continue on despite the setbacks or any disappointments that may come our way. It is the unwavering commitment to never give up, to rise in spite of failure and to keep pushing forward until the goal is achieved.

Persistence is about having a relentless and single-minded

focus on taking consistent actions towards one's goal. It's about tuning out the distractions and maintaining focus the daily grind of achieving a higher level of success. Persistence helps to develop a "stick-to-it" attitude that, over time, delivers results.

Meanwhile, determination is about not just having the will to succeed but also finding a way to make progress when the results seem discouraging. It is the steadfastness of not being pulled down by the negative opinions of others and having faith that the result achieved will be exactly what is meant to be.

The synergy of persistence and determination provides motivational fuel that helps to translate dreams and visions into reality. It helps to propel people into taking action and striving for success. It allows them to believe in their abilities and to withstand the uncertainties and struggles of the journey.

When we are determined and persistent in the pursuit of our dreams, amazing things can happen. We can turn difficult obstacles into stepping-stones to greater achievement and can conjure up the strength and willpower to overcome setbacks. We become bold and fearless in discovering new possibilities and in taking decisive actions.

Ultimately, the importance of persistence and determination towards achieving one's dreams cannot be overstated. It will enable us to stay focused, to remain disciplined, and to find our inner courage during the journey. With this immutable strength, anything becomes possible.

"The only way to reach your goals is to have
the courage to pursue them."

☙

XV

Achieve Your Dreams

It is widely acknowledged that achieving any dream requires discipline, dedication, and hard work. Dreams don't just happen overnight, they may take years of labor and effort. But once that dream has been achieved, a feeling of elation fills the atmosphere. Reaching a goal, whether big or small, is a momentous occasion. Achieving a dream not only demonstrates that hard work pays off, but it can also reveal a newfound sense of confidence in the individual.

For any dream to be achieved, discipline and dedication are of utmost importance. It is a common misconception that dreams can happen without effort, but more often than not, it takes daily practice and dedication to learn certain skills as well as to develop a dedicated mindset. Sometimes having a plan is also a present help, as it allows for individuals to create actionable goals with reasonable timelines to guide them in the right direction. It can be helpful to break down tasks into small, manageable goals that are achievable over a period of time.

Hard work is an indispensable partner in achieving one's dreams. It takes courage, resilience, and dedication to stick to a plan, push through adversity, and never give up. This investment of time and effort can be draining and taxing, but it is vital to remain steady and consistent when building upon a dream. The sense of accomplishment when all the components are put together is worth the grueling hours and weary days.

The importance of attitude must also not be underestimated. Having a positive and optimistic outlook is key when trying to work towards any goal. It is through a consistent change in mindset and outlook that one can keep plugging away, no matter how long it takes, or how difficult the journey may be.

When it comes to achieving any dream, there are a few important things to keep in mind. Firstly, being disciplined, dedicated and having a bit of hard work goes a long way. Secondly, planning, perseverance, and having a positive attitude can prove to be invaluable tools. Thirdly, it is important to establish realistic goals and timelines that can lead you to success. Finally, know that it is often the journey towards a dream that can be the most rewarding thing of all. Even if it takes years, the satisfaction of accomplishing a dream is a feeling like no other.

OTHER BOOKS OF THE AUTHOR

1. The Moments When I Met God
2. Kashiyile Theertha Pathangal
3. GURU GYAN VANI
4. Abhiprerak Gita
5. ASSI SE JAIN GHAT TAK
6. Hopelessness of Arjuna
7. The Soul and It's True Nature
8. Sense of Action (Karma)
9. Action through Wisdom
10. Action through Wisdom
11. THEORY AND PRACTICAL OF EVERY ACTION
12. LOGICAL UNDERSTANDING OF THE SUPREME
13. THE IMPERISHABLE SUPREME
14. Yatra Nishadraj se Hanuman Ghat Tak
15. Yatra Karnatak Ghat se Raja Ghat Tak
16. Yatra Pandey Ghat se Prayagraj Ghat Tak
17. Yatra Ranjendra Prasad Ghat se Dattatreya Ghat Tak
18. YaatraSindhiya Ghat se Gwaliar Ghat Tak
19. Yatra Mangala Gauri Ghat se Hanuman Gadhi Ghat Tak
20. Yatra Gaay Ghat Se Nishad Ghat Tak
21. MAA GANGA, GHATEN EVM UTSAV
22. Ganga Arti Dev Deepavali evam Any Utsav
23. Potentials of Digitalized India
24. VEDIC CONSCIOUSNESS
25. A Brief Introduction to Vedic Science
26. Kashi ke Barah Jyotirling
27. IMPACT OF MOTIVATION
28. Let's have a Milky Way Journey
29. Color Therapy in a Nutshell

30. Rigveda in a Nutshell
31. Yajurveda in a Nutshell
32. Samveda in a Nutshell
33. Atharva Veda in a Nutshell
34. Ayushman Bhava - Ayurveda
35. Srimad Bhagavad Gita and Upanishad Connection
36. Srimad Bhagavad Gita - an attempt to summarize each chapter.
37. Facts and Impact of Nakshatra
38. Astro Gems - NAVARATNA
39. Ekadashi - A Concise Overview
40. A Concise View of Hanuman Chalisa
41. Inspirational Gita
42. Nakshatraranyam
43. Summary of 18 Mahapuranas
44. Synopsis of 18 Upa Puranas
45. Rigvediya Upanishads
46. Shukla Yajurvediya Upanishads
47. Krishna Yajurvediya Upanishads
48. Samavediya Upanishads
49. Atharvavediya Upanishads
50. The Seven Great Sages
51. From Rocket Scientist to President Dr. APJ Abdul Kalam
52. The Visionary's Voice - Quotes of Dr. APJ Abdul Kalam
53. The Wisdom of Swami Vivekananda: Insights and Inspiration from a Legendary Spiritual Teacher
54. Ayurvedic Remedies from the Garden
55. Sages and Seers
56. Rising Strong – Motivational Stories of Women
57. Beyond Flames -Mystery stories of Funeral Ghat Manikarnika
58. The Origins of Tulsi: A Look at the Mythological Roots of the Plant"

Contact

DR. JAGADEESH PILLAI

PhD in Vedic Science

Four Times Guinness World Record Holder

Winner of Mahatma Gandhi Vishwa Shanti Puraskar and
Global Peace Ambassador

Gemology, Astro & Vastu Consultant - Spiritual Counselor

Consultant for designing World Record Ideas

Efficient Tarot Card Reader

9839093003

myrichindia@gmail.com

drjagadeeshpillai@facebook

drjagadeeshpillai@instagram

jagadeeshpillai@youtube

www. JAGADEESHPILLAI.com

ॐ

|| LOKAHA SAMASTHAHA SUKHINO BHAVANTU ||